ME THE TEACHER? NEVER!

HOW TO HOMESCHOOL THROUGH A PANDEMIC AND BEYOND

BY VANESSA HALL, M.ED.

ROYSTON Publishing

BK Royston Publishing
Jeffersonville, IN 47131
http://www.bkroystonpublishing.com
bkroystonpublishing@gmail.com

© Copyright – 2025

All Rights Reserved. No part of this book may be reproduced, stored in a retrieval system, or transmitted by any means without the written permission of the author.

Back Cover Image: Personal Photo

Amplified Bible (AMP) - Copyright © 2015 by The Lockman Foundation, La Habra, CA 90631. All rights reserved.

ISBN-13: 978-1-967282-06-7

Printed in the United States of America

TABLE OF CONTENTS

Introduction	**iv**
Chapter 1	**1**
Where Do You Begin?	
Chapter 2	**2**
Learning Styles	
Chapter 3	**39**
Next Steps	
Chapter 4	**43**
Subject Resources	
References	**49**

INTRODUCTION

As we all know, going through the Covid-19 pandemic was a very trying time. Our children and families were directly impacted in ways we weren't aware of when it started. In March 2020, when the US shutdown for nonessential businesses and schools, it presented a huge undertaking for parents to continue their children's education. It is my goal as an educator and veteran homeschool mother of eighteen years to share with you what has assisted me through my journey. There are many ways to assist moms, dads, grandmas, aunts, etc., in areas concerning each child's education, whether publicly, privately, or even homeschooling during a pandemic.

This writing is a "how to" approach to homeschooling. It is specifically for families who have never assisted with educating their children and includes those who have worked with their child/children before and during early education. You can also create a flexible schedule during the hours that parents work. Please take notes and prepare to glean from the information presented. By the end of this book, you will have a working document you can use with each one of your children.

Homeschooling has been extremely rewarding for my family and thousands of other families as well. Coming from the public and charter school systems in my region to homeschooling was an eye-opening experience. The beginning started at home with my children at a very early age with the alphabet, songs and daily exploring. When they began to get a little older around 3 years old reading kicked in and I wanted more. I started with a homemaker's group of moms, some were homeschooling, and some were just starting like me. I was able to watch their children grasp key concepts and engage in play with one another that truly encouraged me to research further. In all honesty, I still wasn't sure what homeschooling would look like for my household, but I had to go forward in order to find out more for myself. Now all I can say is, WOW! I thank God. He led us in this direction, and I don't regret not one moment. I have the best relationship with my now adult children and my relationship with my husband has blossomed into a forever friendship without the children. Whether you're single or married, you can homeschool your children. I have so many testimonies of personal friends and acquaintances who were successful and you can be too!

1.

WHERE DO YOU BEGIN?

As you prepare to sit down and work through your schedule, the very first thing you need to do is pray. This is not a religious or spiritual book; however, without the Lord involved in your homeschool decision, you will work harder than necessary and struggle. God already knows what each child needs and has chosen you to assist them through their educational career. This is a practical manual that will guide you through each step you'll need to take in order to work with your student/s to ensure success, order, and keep your sanity. Please do not refrain from praying and quieting yourself before God to ask Him for direction, instruction, and order. Regardless of what you believe you are capable of doing on your own, please recognize you would not be reading this book without His leadership and guidance. All you know is not all there is to know. The Bible states it like this in 1 Corinthians 13:9 (AMP): "For we know in part, and we prophesy in part [for our knowledge is fragmentary and incomplete]."

Once you've prayed and quieted yourself, you can set in a great place to learn and apply the tools you'll need for success. These are the beginning tools for our "to-do" book.

2.
LEARNING STYLES

Let's now discuss some of the things you will need to use to evaluate your child/children. Now, you must pay attention to your students during their playtime, studying, writing, and producing what they understand. Let's start with how your student/child learns. What do I mean by how they learn? These are called learning styles; the most common ones are auditory, visual, kinaesthetic*, and read/write (learning by what is seen and written). These styles were taken from an article written by Ricardo Garza, posted on the website Medium on Aug. 2, 2018, "Individual Learning Styles and Learning to Code."

*Kinaesthetic is the British spelling and the U. S. version is spelled Kinesthetic. We will be using the British spelling throughout this book.

Learning Styles

WHAT'S YOUR LEARNING STYLE?

VERBAL
Words are your strongpoint! You prefer to use words both in speech and in writing!

VISUAL
You prefer to use pictures, diagrams, images and spatial understanding to help you learn

MUSICAL / AUDITORY
You prefer using sounds or music or even rhythms to help you learn.

PHYSICAL / KINAESTHETIC
You use your hands, body and sense of touch to help you learn. You might 'act things out'.

LOGICAL / MATHEMATICAL
Learning is easier for you if you use logic, reasoning, systems and sequences.

SOCIAL
You like to learn new things as a part of a group. Explaining your understanding to a group helps you to learn.

SOLITARY
You like to work alone. You use self-study and prefer your own company when learning.

COMBINATION
Your learning style is a combination of two or more of these styles.

Style	Style Defined (Brief description—more details later)
Verbal	They learn by what they are speaking based on what they're seeing.
Visual	They learn from what they are seeing.
Musical/Auditory	They learn from what they are hearing.
Physical/Kinaesthetic	They learn by what they are actively moving and doing.
Logical/Mathematical	They process in an organized form that is rather structured.
Social	They learn well with others.
Solitary	They learn well alone.
Combination	These learners are a combination of two or more learning styles.

Verbal

(Everything that can be helpful about the type of learning - Include what they like, don't like, what typical challenges are, and what positive stimulants are).

A. Likes reading books, articles, i.e. novels, vocabulary etc.

B. Likes researching information via internet etc.

C. Likes learning words via dictionary

D. Likes anything written

E. 2 or more of the above

The verbal style includes both the written and spoken word. If your child uses this style to learn, they will find it easy to express themselves verbally and in writing. They love reading and writing. They like playing on the meaning or sound of words, such as in tongue twisters, rhymes, and limericks. (A limerick is a poem that consists of five lines in a single stanza with a rhyme scheme of AABBA*see page 49. Most limericks are intended to be humorous, and many are considered bawdy, suggestive, or downright indecent, and the like). Children know the meaning of many words and regularly make an effort to find the meaning of new words. They also use these words and phrases they may have recently picked up when talking to others. Reference: learning-style-online.com with some tweaks from me.

Learning and Techniques

If the child/children are verbal learners, try the techniques and ways that involve more speaking and writing practices. For example, help them to talk themselves through procedures in the simulator or use recordings of your content for repetition.

• Make the most of the word-based techniques such as assertions and scripting. Use rhyme and rhythm in your assertions and be sure to read important ones aloud. Set some key points to a familiar song, jingle or theme.

• Mnemonics are an excellent way to help recall lists of information. Acronym mnemonics use words, focusing on the first letter of the word to make up another word or memorable sequence. They can also make up phrases using the items you want to memorize.

- Scripting is also powerful. They don't just have to write them down. They can record scripts using a tape or digital audio recorder (such as an MP3 player) and use it later for reviews.

- When they read content aloud, have them make it dramatic and varied. Instead of using a monotone voice to go over a procedure, turn it into a lively and energetic speech worthy of the theater. Not only does this help their recall, but they can practice their dramatic presence!

- Try using role-playing to learn verbal exchanges such as negotiations, sales, or radio calls.

Notes/Reflections

Notes/Reflections

Visual

(Everything that can be helpful about the type of learning - Include what they like, don't like, what typical challenges are, and what positive stimulants are).

A.   Likes words

B.   Likes reading

C.   Likes writing

D.   Likes spelling, vocabulary

E.   2 or more of the above

If your child uses the visual style, they prefer using images, pictures, colors, and maps to organize information and communicate with others. They can easily visualize objects, plans, and outcomes in their mind. They also have a good spatial sense, which gives them a good sense of direction. They can easily find their way around using maps and rarely get lost. When they walk out of an elevator, they automatically know which way to turn.

Learning and Techniques

- Use images, pictures, color, and other visual media to help them learn. Incorporate much imagery into their visualizations. They may find that visualization comes easily to them. This also means they may have to make some visualizations stand out more than others. This makes sure new material is obvious among all the other visual images they have floating around inside their heads.

- Use color, layout, and spatial organization in their associations, and use many 'visual words' in your assertions. Examples include see, picture, perspective, visual, and map.

- Use mind maps. Wherever possible, use color and pictures in place of text. If they don't use the computer, make sure they have at least four different colored ink pens.

- Systems diagrams can help them visualize the links between parts of a system. Replace words with pictures and use color to highlight major and minor links.

- The visual journey or story technique helps them to memorize content that isn't easy to see. The visual story approach for memorizing procedures is a good example of this.

- Peg words and events come easily to them; however, they will need to spend some time learning at least the first ten peg words. Afterward, their ability to visualize helps them to peg content quickly.

- For more information peg words or if you need further information, please sign up for my monthly learning sessions. See page 39 for more details.

Notes/Reflections

Notes/Reflections

Musical/Auditory/Aural

(Everything that can be helpful about the type of learning - Include what they like, don't like, what typical challenges are, and what positive stimulants are).

A.   Likes to record the lesson

B.   Likes to talk out loud, answer questions verbally

C.   Likes music in the background or some type of sound

D.   Likes audio books

E.   2 or more of the above

Aural style is defined as relating to the ear or the sense of hearing. If your child uses the aural style, they usually like to work with sound and music. They have a good sense of pitch and rhythm. They typically can sing, play a musical instrument, or identify the sounds of different instruments. Certain music invokes strong emotions. They will notice the music playing in the background of movies, TV shows, and other media. They often find themselves humming or tapping a song or jingle without any prompting. If your child/children are aural learners, they use sound, rhyme, and music in their learning. Focus on using aural content in their association and visualization.

Learning and Techniques

- Use sound recordings to provide a background and help them get into visualizations. For example, use a recording of a particular item you're covering, playing loudly via a headset, to practice those procedures or instructions. If you don't have these recordings, consider creating them.

- When creating mnemonics or acrostics, make the most of rhythm and rhyme, or set them to a jingle or part of a song.

- If there is a particular music or song that makes them want to 'take on the world,' play it back and help them align their emotions and state of mind. When they need the boost, they can easily recall that state of mind without needing the music.

Notes/Reflections

Notes/Reflections

Physical/Kinaesthetic

(Everything that can be helpful about the type of learning - Include what they like, don't like, what typical challenges are, and what positive stimulants are).

A. **Likes doing things, i.e. legos, robotics etc.**

B. **Likes acting out events, i.e. play therapy, drama etc.**

C. **Likes to move about i.e. sports, dance, etc.**

D. **Likes to act out the reading lessons, etc.**

E. **2 or more of the above**

If your child uses the physical style, it's likely they use their body and sense of touch to learn about the world around them. It's likely they like sports and exercise, as well as other physical activities such as working with their hands, e.g. Legos or woodworking. They like to think out issues, ideas, and problems while they exercise. They would rather go for a run or walk if something is bothering them rather than sitting at home. They are more sensitive to the physical world around them. They notice and appreciate textures, for example, in clothes or furniture. They like getting their hands dirty, making models, or working out jigsaws. Typically, they use larger hand gestures and other body language to communicate. They probably don't mind getting up and dancing either, at least when the time is right. They either love the physical action of theme park rides or it upsets their inner body sense too much, so they avoid them altogether. When learning a new skill or topic, they prefer to 'jump in' and play with the physical parts as soon as possible. They would prefer to pull an engine apart and put it back together rather than read or look at diagrams about how it works. The thought of sitting in a lecture listening to someone else talk is repulsive. In those circumstances, they fidget or can't sit still for long. They want to get up and move around.

Learning and Techniques

Use touch, action, movement, and hands-on work in your learning activities if you use a physical style. For visualization, focus on the sensations you would expect in each scenario. For example, if you visualize a tack (turn) on a sailboat, focus on physical sensations. Describe the feeling of the pressure against their hand as they turn the rudder and the tension lessening on the ropes. Help them sense how the wind changes to the other side, feel the thud as the sail swaps with the wind, and feel the boat speed up as they start the new leg.

- For assertions and scripting, describe the physical feelings of your actions. For example, a pilot might script as follows: "I feel the friction as I push the throttle forward to start my takeoff run. The controls start to feel more responsive as I check the airspeed, oil pressure, and temperature. At takeoff speed, I pull back slightly, and I feel the vibrations of the wheels stop as the plane leaves the ground. After a few moments, I reach down and set the gear selector to up. I feel the satisfying bump as the gear stops fully up."
- Use physical objects as much as possible. Allow the child/children to physically touch objects as they learn about what they do. Flashcards can help them memorize information because they can touch and move them around.
- Keep in mind as well that writing and drawing diagrams are physical activities, so don't neglect these techniques. Perhaps use big sheets of paper and large color markers for your diagrams. You then get more action from the drawing.

- Teach the child/children to use breathing and relaxation to focus their state while they learn and perform. They should focus on staying calm, centered, relaxed, and aware. If you want them to gain more control over their physical state, look up some references on autogenic training. This was a secret behind the great Russian athletic performances over the past few decades.

Notes/Reflections

Notes/Reflections

Logical/Mathematical

(Everything that can be helpful about the type of learning - Include what they like, don't like, what typical challenges are, and what positive stimulants are).

A. **Learning is easier for you if you use logic, reasoning systems and sequences.**

B. **Math is one of the methods that is used because of the way the learner grabs information.**

If your child/children use the logical learning style, they like using their brain for logical and mathematical reasoning. They can recognize patterns easily and connections between seemingly meaningless content. This also leads them to classify and group information to help them learn or understand it. They work well with numbers and can perform complex calculations. They remember the basics of trigonometry and algebra and can do moderately complex calculations in their head. They typically work through problems and issues in a systematic way and like to create procedures for future use. They are happy setting numerical targets and budgets and tracking their progress toward these. They enjoy creating agendas, itineraries, and to-do lists and typically number and rank them before putting them into action. Your child/children with a scientific approach to thinking will often support points with logical examples or statistics. They pick up logical flaws in other people's words, writing, or actions and may point these out to people (not always to everyone's amusement). They like working out strategies and using simulation. They may enjoy games such as brainteasers, backgammon, and chess. They may also like computer games such as Dune II, StarCraft, Age of Empires, Sid Meier games, and others.

Learning and Techniques

- Aim to understand the reasons behind their content and skills. Don't just rote learn. Understanding more detail behind their compulsory content helps them memorize and learn the material they need to know. Have them explore the links between various systems and make a note of them.
- While they study, have them create and use lists by extracting key points from their material. They may also want to use statistics and other analyses to help identify areas for specific concentration.
- Pay attention to their physical state, for example, their breathing and stress level. They may isolate their own body from their rational thought. Help them remember that they are just as much a part of the *system* as any equipment they use.
- Also, point out that association often works well when it is illogical. It doesn't matter how logical two items are together. They have a better chance of recalling them later if they have made the association illogical. Their brain may protest at first!
- In their scripting, though, have them highlight logical thoughts and behaviors. Highlighting increases their ability to pick up systems and procedures easily, which can be detected when they need to change a set procedure.

Notes/Reflections

Notes/Reflections

Social

(Everything that can be helpful about the type of learning - Include what they like, don't like, what typical challenges are, and what positive stimulants are).

If you have a child/children with a strong social style, they communicate well with people, both verbally and nonverbal. People listen to them or come to them for advice, and they're sensitive to other's motivations, feelings, or moods. They listen well and understand other's views. They may enjoy mentoring or counseling others. They typically prefer learning in groups or classes or spending one-on-one time with a teacher or instructor. Their learning is heightened by bouncing their thoughts off others and listening to how others respond. They prefer to work through issues, ideas, and problems with a group. They thoroughly enjoy working with a clicking or synergistic group and prefer to stay around after class and talk with others. Social activities are of high interest rather than doing their own thing. They prefer playing games involving other people, such as card games and board games. The same applies to team sports such as football or soccer, basketball, baseball, volleyball, baseball and hockey.

Learning and Techniques

- Direct social learners to work with others as much as possible. Encourage them to study with a class. If this is not available, then consider forming your own study group with others at a similar level. They don't have to be from the same school or class. If you like, introduce them to some of the techniques from this book. It may be easier for you to try some of the Memetic Techniques in a social setting and work with the feedback from others. Memetic Technique is an idea, behavior, style, or usage that spreads from person to person within a culture.

• Role-playing is a technique that works well with others, whether it's one-on-one or with a group of people. For example, in aviation training, role-play the aerodrome area. Have people walking around in circuits making the right radio calls with the tower coordinating everyone. Another example might be role-playing with one person being the instructor and the other being the student.

• Encourage them to work on some of their associations and visualizations with other people. Make sure they understand the principles of what they are doing though: Otherwise, you may get some interesting responses! Others often have different perspectives and creative styles, so the group may come up with more varied and imaginative associations compared to the ones you might create.

• Rather than allowing child/children to recite assertions to themselves, try having them share their key assertions with others. By doing so, they are almost signing a social contract that their assertion is what they do. This strengthens their assertions.

Notes/Reflections

Notes/Reflections

Solitary

(Everything that can be helpful about the type of learning - Include what they like, don't like, what typical challenges are, and what positive stimulants are).

- You like to work alone and sometimes in complete silence. Noise may be an overload and cause you to be distracted.

- You'd prefer not to be in a group and sometimes children may "act out" due to this fact.

If you have a solitary type of child/children, they are more private, introspective, and independent. Solitary types can concentrate well, focusing their thoughts and feelings on the current topic(s). They are aware of their thoughts and may analyze the different ways they think and feel. Naturally, they spend time on self-analysis and often reflect on past events and how they approach them. Because they feel they know themselves, thinking independently and understanding their mind is also instinctive. They take time to ponder and assess their accomplishments or challenges. Some keep a journal, diary, or personal log to record their thoughts and events. Spending time alone is enjoyable for them, especially if they have a hobby. They prefer traveling to or vacationing in remote places away from crowds. They may have attended self-development workshops, read self-help books, or used other methods to develop a deeper understanding of themself. Their preferred approach to problems is to retreat somewhere quiet and work through possible solutions. Sometimes, they spend too much time trying to solve a problem that could more easily be solved by talking to someone. They like to make plans, set goals and know their direction in life and work. If they don't know their current direction in life, they feel a deep sense of dissatisfaction. Self-employment is most attractive to them or they may have thought a lot about it.

Learning and Techniques

Some children prefer to learn alone using self-study; consequently, they may dislike learning in groups. When they spend time with an instructor or a teacher, they often only clarify information they could not clarify themselves.

- Encourage solitary learners to ask questions like: What's in this for me? Why does this matter? and How can I use this idea?'
- Teach them to know their inner thoughts and feelings towards various topics. This is because their inner thoughts impact their motivation and ability to learn more than they do in the other styles. Here are a few ideas for you as the homeschool teacher that will help this along:
- Spend more time on the Target step of the Memetic Approach. Encourage children to set their goals, objectives, and plans. Define ultra-clear visualizations or scripts of what life is like once they have achieved their goals. Understand their reasons for undertaking each objective and ensure they are happy with their learning goals.
- Help them align their goals and objectives with personal beliefs and values. If there is misalignment, they may run into issues with motivation or confidence. It's not always obvious what the underlying cause is. If you suspect a misalignment, try some of the techniques like *five whys and seventy by seven* to flush these issues out. Scripting and assertions also help highlight issues. If they script their goal and find they don't like certain parts of it, that's probably a hint that it has some misalignment.
- Create a personal interest in your topics. Attract their attention by connecting them to realistic objects that interests them. For example, if there is an interest in becoming a pilot, introduce them to current and past aviators. Ask questions like:

Why do others find aviation interesting? What is in it for them? What keeps them motivated? Why do they work in the field? You may also want to look at the authors behind your books or teaching material. What was their motivation to create it? Why do you think they organized the material in the way they did? Can you ask the authors their motives behind their methods? You might want to email or have your older students write them for answers to some of these questions.

- Encourage solitary learners to keep a log or journal. One separate journal from their normal journal or training log could be advantageous when it includes extra information about their thoughts and feelings about the homeschool teaching program and outcomes. Suggest they outline challenges, ideas on how to overcome them, and what worked. Tell them to write down what works well and doesn't work well for them. While they are studying, encourage them to be aware of thoughts or concerns that arise and write them down, highlight items, or mark them in a way that makes finding them easier. If needed, concerns can be discussed with others, bearing in mind it may be more efficient to put something confusing aside and ask others later. This is often better than spending too much time trying to work it out themselves.

- When solitary learners associate and visualize, suggest they highlight their thoughts and feelings at the time. They may want to do most of their visualization and association in private. Advise them also to try talking to others with more experience to get an idea of their thoughts and feelings in various circumstances.

- Assertions are important for them. Solitary learners drive themselves by the way they see themselves internally. Assertions are a good way to ensure internal self-image matches learning objectives. This also applies to the scripting techniques, so advise learners to include internal thinking and feelings in their scripts.

- Modeling is a powerful technique for solitary learners. Don't just model behaviors and appearance for the learners, try to *get inside their heads* and model the thought patterns and feelings you believe the child/children have in various circumstances. You can gain ideas by talking to people or reading biographies. Remember, you don't have to find a single perfect model. Create a model that combines several people.

- Be creative with role-playing. You don't always need others to role-play with because you can create plenty of people using visualization! For example, you can visualize your instructor beside you or a colleague and you practicing a procedure or skill. Work with them and talk to them while you visualize. An advantage of this form of role-playing is that you can control their behavior!

- When changing behaviors and habits, you need to have a strong desire to make the changes you want. Explore the benefits of making a change and visualize scenarios in which you've already made the change. If you don't believe strongly in the benefits, you may find it difficult to change the behavior.

- Your thoughts significantly influence your performance and safety. Thoughts are just as much a part of a system as the physical equipment you use, such as an aircraft, car, or boat. In addition, other people are also part of those systems, so be aware that their thoughts and feelings can affect the overall system.

- **Refine the reliability of your system.** Years of refinement have made physical equipment such as aircrafts and boats safe and reliable. For example, aircraft failure causes less than ten percent of all aircraft accidents. The largest percentage is pilot error, more than seventy percent. This is likely the case in many other fields. It's just not as visible when accidents happen. Thus, it's well worthwhile spending some time refining your systems.

Notes/Reflections

Notes/Reflections

Combination

(Everything that can be helpful about the type of learning - Include what they like, don't like, what typical challenges are, and what positive stimulants are).

- Two or more of these learning styles may be combined.

Everyone has a mix of learning styles. Some people may find they have a dominant learning style with far less use of other styles. Others may find that they use different styles in different circumstances. There is no right mix. Nor are your styles fixed. You can develop your ability in less dominant styles, as well as further develop styles that you already use well. By recognizing and understanding your learning styles, you can use techniques better suited to you. This improves the speed and quality of your learning.

Notes/Reflections

Notes/Reflections

3.
Next Steps

Once you have gone through these learning styles, I am confident you can choose the appropriate educational curriculum materials for your student/s. I have developed a quiz for you to take, which will assist you with determining which learning style and materials you will need to choose for your student/s. Once the quiz is completed, the resource-by-subject list will direct you to the appropriate curriculum. I designed it by grade and subject so that it will be easy for you to locate the proper grade and then read across for the information to determine and finalize.

You are welcome to join my online monthly learning sessions for more information and support. As an online member, you will receive the quiz for you to discover your child/children, student/students unique learning style as well as daily blogs and monthly support. For more details, visit http://www.thehallsway2educate.com.

Notes/Reflections

Notes/Reflections

Notes/Reflections

4.
RESOURCES BY SUBJECT

Grade	Subject	Suggested Learner and Why	Suggested Curriculum	Contact Resource for Purchasing
K4-6th grades 4-12 year olds	All Subjects	All Learning Styles	Foundations/Essentials/Challenge	www.classicalconversations.com
K5-10th grades 5-15 year olds	Math	Verbal/Visual Learner	Verbal Math	Michael Levin www.Amazon.com
K-6th grades 5-12 year olds	Math	Auditory Learner	Math Lessons for a Living Education	www.rainbowresource.com
1st-6th grades 6-12 year olds	Math	Read/Write/Verbal/Visual	Kumon	www.rainbowresource.com
5th-8th grades 10-13 year olds	Math	Kinaesthetic	Hands-On Equations Fractions Learning System	www.rainbowresource.com
K-6th grades 5-12 year olds	Math	All Learning Styles	MCP Math Level K,A,B,C,D,E and F	www.rainbowresource.com
K-12th grades 5-18 year olds	Math	Verbal/Visual/Read Write/ Kinaesthetic Learning Styles	Saxon	www.hmhco.com
K-12th grades 5-18 year olds	Math	Verbal/Visual/Kinaesthetic	Math U See	www.mathusee.com

ME THE TEACHER? NEVER! | 43

Grade	Subject	Suggested Learner and Why	Suggested Curriculum	Contact Resource for Purchasing
K5-1st grades 5-6 year olds	Reading Vocab	Verbal/Visual	Cut and Paste Vocabulary Sentences	www.rainbowresource.com
All grades and All ages	Reading	Verbal/Visual Learner	All About Reading	www.allaboutlearningpress.com
K-12th grades 5-18 year olds	Vocab Reading	Verbal/Visual/ Read/Write	Megawords	www.rainbowresource.com
1st-6th grades 6-12 year olds	Reading	Verbal/Visual/ Auditory	Worldly Wise 3000	www.rainbowresource.com
PreK-1st grades 4-6 year olds	Reading	Verbal/Visual Kinaesthetic Read/Write	The Critical Thinking Co.	www.rainbowresource.com
3rd grade-Ad 8 yr.-Adult	English/ Reading	Verbal/Visual/ Read/Kinaesthetic	Logic of English Multi-Level	www.Essentials.logicofenglish.com
1st-8th grades 6-13 year olds	English Language	Verbal/Visual/ Read/Write	The Well Trained Mind Jessie	www.well-trainedmind.com
K4-12th grades 4-18 year olds	English Writing	Verbal/Visual/ Read/Write	Classical Conversations	www.classicalconversations.com

Grade	Subject	Suggested Learner and Why	Suggested Curriculum	Contact Resource for Purchasing
K4-12 years old	Science	Combination Learning Styles	Science Around the Year- Janice VanCleave 201 Awesome Magical Bizarre & Incredible Experiments	www.classicalconversations.com www.rainbowresource.com
K4-12 years old	Science	Auditory/ Musical	Lyrical Life Science. Vol. 1 Lyrical Life Science Vol. 2 Lyrical Life Science Vol. 3	www.rainbowresource.com www.classicalconversations.com
K-6th grade	Science	Visual/Verbal/ Kinaesthetic Read/Write	Zoology Volumes 1-3 Botany Textbook and Notebook Sets	www.rainbowresource.com www.apologia.com
7th & 8th grade	Science	Visual/Verbal/ Kinaesthetic/ Read/Write	Earth Science General Science Textbook and Notebook Sets	www.rainbowresource.com www.apologia.com
9th grade	Science	Verbal/Visual Kinaesthetic Read/Write	Physical Science Textbook and Notebook Set	www.rainbowresource.com www.apologia.com
9th-12th grades	Science	Visual/Verbal/ Read/Write	High School Astronomy	www.apologia.com
K-6th	History/ Social Studies	Visual/Verbal Read/Write Kinaesthetic	Classical Acts and Facts History Cards Trivium at the Table Placemats Visual History of the World	www.classicalconversationsbooks.com www.rainbowresource.com

Grade	Subject	Learning Style	Resources	Websites
7th-8th	History/ Social Studies	Visual/Verbal Read/Write Kinaesthetic	Classical Acts and Facts History Cards Visual History of the World	www.classicalconversationsbooks.com www.rainbowresource.com
9th-12th	History/ Social Studies	Visual/Verbal Read/Write Kinaesthetic	Eat Your Way Around the World Cartography Heroes of History	www.rainbowresource.com www.classicalconversationsbooks.com www.rainbowresource.com

Notes/Reflections

Notes/Reflections

5.
REFERENCES

https://www.rasmussen.edu/degrees/education/blog/types-of-learning-styles/

https://www.learning-style-online.com

https://vark-learn.com/introduction-to-vark/the-vark-modalities/

www.classicalconversations.com

www.rainbowresource.com

AABBA - https://www.masterclass.com/articles/poetry-101-what-is-a-rhyme-scheme-learn-about-rhymed-poems-with-examples

Notes/Reflections

Notes/Reflections

www.ingramcontent.com/pod-product-compliance
Lightning Source LLC
Chambersburg PA
CBHW042003150426
43194CB00002B/109